IMAGES
of England

MARPLE
AND
MELLOR

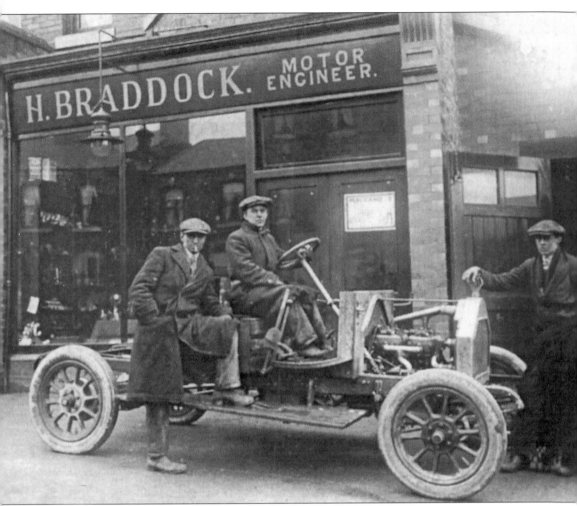

BRADDOCK'S GARAGE, STOCKPORT ROAD, 1920s.

IMAGES
of England

MARPLE
AND
MELLOR

Compiled by
Ann Hearle

TEMPUS

First published 1997, reprinted 2001
Copyright © Ann Hearle, 1997

Tempus Publishing Limited
The Mill, Brimscombe Port,
Stroud, Gloucestershire, GL5 2QG

ISBN 0 7524 0316 8

Typesetting and origination by
Tempus Publishing Limited
Printed in Great Britain by
Midway Colour Print, Wiltshire

Contents

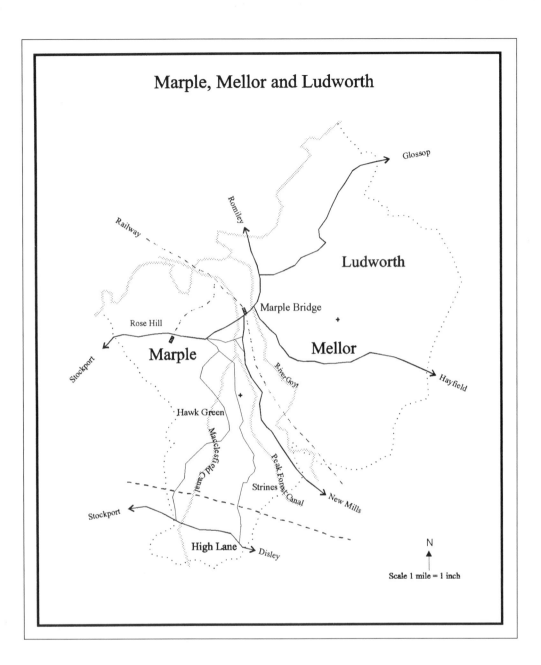

Marple, Mellor and Ludworth

Glossop

Romiley

Railway

Ludworth

Rose Hill

Marple Bridge

Marple

Mellor

Stockport

River Goyt

Hayfield

Hawk Green

Macclesfield Canal

Peak Forest Canal

Strines

New Mills

Stockport

High Lane

Disley

N

Scale 1 mile = 1 inch

Introduction

Marple today is made up of a small town, several villages and scattered hamlets within the south-east boundary of the conurbation of Greater Manchester. It has a population of just over 24,000. The district covers an area of slightly more than 11 square miles, (7,000 acres) and rises from around 300 ft at the lowest point on the River Goyt to just over one 1,000 ft on Cobden Edge.

From the time of the Saxons, when counties were established, Mellor and Ludworth were in Derbyshire and Marple was in Cheshire, with the boundary formed by the Rivers Goyt and Etherow. In 1895 Marple Urban District Council was established and in 1936, Mellor and Ludworth were, not without opposition, 'moved' from Derbyshire into Cheshire and became part of the Marple Urban District. However, in 1974 the council ceased to exist and the area is now part of the Stockport Metropolitan Borough in the County of Greater Manchester. Now, except for the school and the Women's Institute, Ludworth is an almost forgotten name because the post office call much of it, and also parts of Mellor and Lower Marple, Marple Bridge.

About the same time as the counties were formed, the ecclesiastical parish system came into existence and played an enormous part in the day-to-day life of the villages, or townships as they were then known. Marple was a chapelry in the Parish of Stockport in the Diocese of Chester, whilst Mellor and Ludworth formed the Chapelry of Mellor in the Parish of Glossop in the enormous Diocese of Lichfield. Marple, now two parishes, is still in the Diocese of Chester. Mellor Parish, which still includes Ludworth, is in the Diocese of Derby - the one remaining link with its old county.

Originally an area of scattered hamlets and farms, the people supplemented their incomes with the production of home-produced hand-made textiles. There were only two families of gentry, the Bradshaw/Isherwoods of Marple

Hall and the Chethams of Mellor Hall. In the last quarter of the eighteenth century, one large and several small water-powered cotton spinning mills were erected in Mellor. The builder of the largest mill was Samuel Oldknow. He changed the face of the whole area with his mill, roads, the Peak Forest Canal, lime kilns, coal mines, workers' housing and modern farms. However, no other large mill was constructed in Marple until the Hollins in the 1830s. This mill, and the streets built around it, became the present centre of Marple. The families - the Carvers and the Hodgkinsons - who owned and ran the company, had a tremendous impact on the growth of the village and influenced every activity, whether social, religious, educational, political or recreational, for a hundred years. In the middle of the last century over half of the working people earned their living in the textile industry, and a quarter in the mines, quarries and farms.

Most of the mills and coal mines in Mellor had closed by the 1880s and this had left the village with a reduction of almost half its population by the end of the century. In 1881, over a hundred houses were lying empty, mostly in Moor End, where the Dove Bank Mills had gone up in flames in the 1870s. Then, in 1892, the Mellor Mill, which had employed over 500 people at its peak, burnt down, causing further unemployment in the district.

Ludworth's population remained static over the nineteenth century and, whilst Marple grew, it did not expand as fast as the surrounding cotton towns; the area was not an industrial or commercial success! Some time after the arrival of the railway in 1862, villas, large and small, for the new commuters, business men and their clerks, started to be built in Marple, Mellor and Ludworth. There was some growth in the first half of this century but the major expansion, mostly in Marple, occurred in the building of estates, private and council, in the 1960s. Further growth is now constrained by the Green Belt, so it looks as if the beauty of the hills, the canals, and the fields will remain for the enjoyment of all.

Just before the Second World War some of the old stone built houses and cottages were demolished in the cause of 'slum' clearance. The early post-war years saw the disappearance of Marple and Brabyns Halls, along with a number of other buildings. If only they had survived a few more decades, they would all have become 'highly desirable'! The remaining old farms, houses and cottages are now 'renovated and modernised' and eagerly sought after.

Over two hundred photographs are included in the book, many of which have never appeared in print before. They are mostly from my own collection, gathered over nearly thirty years of living in Mellor. A good number of the others come from the Marple Local History Society, of which I am the chairman. Others have been lent to me by local people, for which I am very grateful, and I have tried to include all their names in the acknowledgements.

One
Dan Bank to the Centre

MARPLE HALL, 1959.

Seventeen Windows, Marple.

SEVENTEEN WINDOWS, OFFERTON. Seen here in the early 1900s, the building is not actually in Marple but is regarded by most people as the entrance to the town. The house is now just a shadow of its former self - all that is left after a disastrous fire in the early 1940s. In the last century hand-loom silk weavers worked in the loft behind the row of attic windows.

TOLL HOUSE, DAN BANK. The house, shown here in the early 1900s, stood on the corner of Dooley Lane and Dan Bank, on the road from Stockport to New Mills. Marple starts at this cross roads. Samuel Oldknow made the improvements to the road in 1797, and it was turnpiked in 1801. The house remained until the mid 1920s when it was demolished during road widening works. (See page 109)

DOOLEY LANE COTTAGES, EARLY 1900s. This row of late eighteenth century cottages includes the Hare and Hounds. Today only the public house is still standing. In the late 1950s, first the cottages on the far side were demolished and then the two on this side were pulled down. This allowed the road to be 'moved' from the river side to its present position, removing a dangerous bend, which had led to a number of accidents.

DOOLEY LANE ENTRANCE TO MARPLE HALL. In the early 1900s, when this picture was taken, the gates were at the start of one of the carriage drives to the hall. A more modest gate is in its place today. The front gates on the Stockport Road were much grander, but those too have gone.

MARPLE HALL, 1850. This print shows the back of the hall from the ornamental lake at the foot of the cliff. Parts of the original Cheshire farmhouse were incorporated into the new hall, which was built by Henry Bradshaw in 1659. This was after the Civil War but before the restoration of the monarchy in 1660. Henry's son, another Henry, added the stables and barns and further alterations were made at the start of the last century. The estate passed through the female line from the Bradshaws to the Isherwoods in the eighteenth century and was the main home of the family for over three hundred years, although the house was seldom occupied after the death of the old squire, John, in 1920. A three day sale in 1929 saw the dispersal of most of the furniture, tapestries and china. The hall, looked after by a caretaker, was open to the public and available for parties for a number of years before and after the sale. After the departure of the caretaker it was increasingly vandalised and 'stripped'. In 1959, in a dangerous condition, it was demolished by Marple Council. What a loss!

THE STABLES, MARPLE HALL, 1959. There were numerous outbuildings around the hall, including stables, barns and coach houses. Several had cottages built into them for the staff. All were demolished along with the hall itself.

ROSE HILL COTTAGES, 1890s. These half timbered cottages stood on the Stockport Road above Rose Hill Station. Silk hand-loom weavers inhabited them for many years; in 1851 there were eleven weavers living there. In 1875 the estate, with the old Rose Hill House and cottages, was bought by Samuel Hodgkinson. The cottages and the adjoining warehouse were demolished to make way for a new drive and a gatehouse. (See page 108)

BOWDEN LANE. Seen here from the Stockport Road end in the early 1900s, the lane has now been widened but has changed little from the time of the photograph. The young man in the foreground appears to be holding cans of milk, no doubt collected from one of the nearby farms. There were over eighty dairy farms in the area just after the Second World War. The two gentlemen would not stand in the middle of the road today!

THE POND ON BOWDEN LANE, EARLY 1900s. The new villas built along the lane were for the clerks who travelled by train to their offices in Stockport and Manchester. The view looking over the pond is towards the Stockport Road; the back of the houses on that road can be seen on the far left.

NAB TOP SANATORIUM, 1920s. In 1912 a nursing home was established at Nab Top; eight years later it became a sanatorium for tuberculosis patients sent by the Salford Corporation and by 1929, it had 120 beds for people in the early stages of the disease. Marple had a reputation for being a healthy place. After the National Health Service was established in 1947, the sanatorium became the Dale Hospital and was also used for patients with other types of illness. It was closed in 1981.

CRIPPLED CHILDREN'S NURSING HOME, 1920s. In 1907 a seven-roomed cottage on Cross Lane was rented by the Manchester and Salford Cripples Aid Society to be used as a holiday home for crippled children. There, cared for by nurses, they could have a fortnight's holiday. In 1914 new purpose built premises were opened on Dale Road. This later became the Children's Orthopaedic Hospital for long stay patients. Schooling was also provided. It is easy today to forget just how many children were crippled from diseases such as polio and rickets.

COTTAGES BY THE JOLLY SAILOR. Now all gone, these eighteenth century cottages and early nineteenth century terrace are shown here in the at the start of this century. They used to stand next to the Jolly Sailor, where there is now a parade of shops. All the houses, which included one small front room shop, were demolished in the 'slum' clearances of 1936.

NORBURY SMITHY, EARLY 1900s. The area near the Jolly Sailor was known as Norbury Smithy for centuries. It was the biggest hamlet in Marple before the present town centre developed with the building of Hollins Mill. (See page 108) What is now the centre of Marple was once farms, fields and a few cottages. In the doorway can be seen Mr Wood, the smithy.

PEACE FARM AND BARN, 1930s. Also gone, it stood where the Texaco garage now stands. The farm was the first home of the Bradshaws of Marple Hall after they moved from Derbyshire. It was the birth place of John Bradshaw, the judge. The house, originally known as 'The Place', and barn were demolished in 1936. Behind it, Shirley Avenue was built to rehouse people made homeless by the demolition of the 'slums'. One old lady, from the cottages by the Jolly Sailor, was allowed to start a little shop in her new house to replace the one she had lost.

JUNCTION OF CHURCH LANE AND STOCKPORT ROAD. Where there is now a small patch of greenery at the junction of these roads, there used to be another smithy. It is said that there were three smithies in the area at one time. The photograph, taken on Church Lane in the late 1930s, shows the entrance to the smithy and a jumble of buildings. At the back, on the left, can be seen the open area which was left vacant after the demolition of the cottages by the Jolly Sailor. (See previous page) For many years it was used as a site for markets and visits from travelling fun fairs.

STOCKPORT ROAD AND HOLLINS MILL. Just past the Jolly Sailor, seen on the left of this photograph taken in the early 1900s, is the start of Station Road, with Bowden's grocery shop (now Chiu's Chinese takeaway) on the other corner. The chimney and six-storey spinning building of Hollins Mill dominates the area opposite Market Street. In its most prosperous times several hundred people would have worked there. (See page 108)

Two

Hawk Green, the Ridge and the Lakes

PEACEFIELD COTTAGES, CROSS LANE, *c.* 1905.

CROSS LANE COTTAGES. Seen here in the early 1900s, this beautiful old building, demolished in the clearances of 1936, is another of Marple's losses. There is a plaque with the date 1702 over one of the windows, but the house was probably rebuilt at this date and would probably have contained pieces of an earlier timber built house.

WOODVILLE FARM, EARLY 1900s. Part of this house, formerly called Bridges Farm, still exists on Buxton Lane. The farmhouse and its land were bought by John Carver (See page 108) in the 1860s and Woodville, a large house with stables and ornamental gardens was built. The farm land was built on after the Second World War.

WOODVILLE, EARLY 1900s. Built of yellow brick, it a was a substantial house, befitting one of the owners of Hollins Mill. John Carver and his wife, Hannah, raised their children here before moving to Ealing in Middlesex. It is said that Hannah did not like the connection with 'trade'! Woodville was then occupied by the Hodgkinson and Barlow families before becoming a council nursing home in the 1960s. It has recently been demolished and a new private nursing home has been built on the site. (See page 108)

DEMOLITION OF WOODVILLE, 1995.

BARNSFOLD MANOR. Taken in the late 1880s, this is one of the earliest photographs of the area. Barnsfold is a group of old houses near Hawk Green dating back centuries. The fields nearby are the only mention of Marple in the Domesday Book. Part of the house is dated 1658, a year earlier than Marple Hall, so there must have been settled conditions in the area just before the restoration of the monarchy in 1660 for people to have the confidence to rebuild. There are traces of a yet earlier building incorporated into its construction. It is very little changed today.

HAWK GREEN. Outside the Crown in the early 1900s, what are the people watching? All the men and even the boys are wearing hats. It must have been a sunny day as some of the men are wearing boaters. The ladies are using umbrellas as parasols.

THE RIDGE METHODIST CHAPEL. Seen here in the early 1900s, this large chapel built in 1874, could seat 440 people and was called 'the Cathedral of the North'. It was demolished because of dry rot and a decrease in members in the late 1960s. The small building on the left was the original chapel, erected in 1844, which was used as a Sunday School during the lifetime of the big chapel. It is now, refurbished, the chapel once again. (See page 87)

ALL SAINTS AND THE ROUND HOUSE, *c.* 1890s. Only the tower of the old church, the carriage and hearse houses remain. The church was built in 1812, mostly through the efforts and money of Samuel Oldknow, to replace a derelict wooden one. (See page 109) A new church was built alongside in 1878 because the Georgian building was not strong enough to take the proposed new aisles. The chancel and nave of the Oldknow church were pulled down in 1964 because they were in a dangerous condition. The Round House may have been built as a toll house but the road was never turnpiked. It was demolished during this century.

THE GEORGIAN CHURCH IN RUINS, 1963. This is the interior of the Georgian church just prior to demolition. In the middle of the last century the area to the left was the Bradshaw/Isherwood enclosed pew. The door had a large coat of arms on it and the area was carpeted, with an easy chair, a table, cushioned seats, a fireplace and curtains for privacy. The dogs accompanied the family to church!

THE SHANTY, CHURCH LANE, 1931. Built in the 1890s in the Arts and Crafts style, the Shanty featured in a lecture, subsequently printed, by one of the architects, Raymond Unwin, entitled *The Art of Designing Small Houses and Cottages.*

WHIT WALK PASSING ALL SAINTS' SCHOOL. In 1831, the first children of All Saints' School met in the upper barn of Chapel House Farm for lessons. (See next page) They moved to the new school in 1838. The large procession passing the school, complete with banner, is that of one of the Whit Walks in the early 1900s. In their new clothes, the children and adults of the church would process around the village before returning to a tea. The land to the right of the stone wall had not yet been built on.

CHAPEL HOUSE FARM, 1965. This large group of buildings was also known as Colliers Fold. Part of the estate was bought in 1787 by Samuel Oldknow - one of his first acquisitions in Marple. He bought the rest in 1791. In the 1980s the farm was sold and the buildings were extensively modernised and combined to form one large house.

STRINES ROAD. In the early 1900s this was a very empty road, with no vehicles, no houses and just a few people watching the photographer. Strines Road was constructed as a completely new section for the Stockport to New Mills turnpike in the late eighteenth century. Oldknow's original plan was for the road to go past his Mellor Mill on the Derbyshire side of the river.

SPOUT HOUSE, STRINES ROAD. Seen here in the early 1900s, these cottages, not much altered, still exist today. Joel Wainwright, writing at the end of the last century, said that James Wadsworth of Spout House was the inventor of the 'first domestic washing machine and mangle combined'. He doesn't record if it was a commercial success.

CRUCK BARN, STRINES ROAD, 1962. This barn, in an advanced state of dereliction, has two curved beams that form an 'A' shape. This is the cruck form of building in wood. It was repaired and extended to make a home in the 1970s. In the background can be seen the Victorian house called the Grange.

TURF LEA COTTAGES, *c.* 1905. Many of the people living below the Ridge, at Turf Lea, were employed by the nearby Strines Print Works.

Tea Gardens, Roman Lakes, Marple

THE TEA GARDENS AT THE ROMAN LAKES, EARLY 1900s. After Mellor Mill, which stood in the valley below the Strines Road, was burnt down in 1892, the estate was run by the mill manager as a tourist venue. The old mill ponds were renamed the Roman Lakes to attract trippers from the nearby towns. There were boats for hire, tea rooms, slot machines, postcards for sale, and even a dance floor. Thousands of people visited, especially on Bank Holidays. (See page 109)

FLOODGATE COTTAGES. To cater for all the visitors to the area many tea rooms were opened up. (See pages 102 and 104). Floodgate Cottages, near the railway viaduct, had a large wooden tea room erected which can be seen in the centre of this picture, taken in the early 1900s. Apart from the disappearance of the tea room, the scene is still the same today.

MARSHALL'S TEA ROOMS. This postcard from the early 1900s shows the tea rooms and cottages at Floodgate from the other side. Over the wall on the right is the weir, which diverted water from the River Goyt to the mill ponds. These supplied the water that powered the three large water wheels of Mellor Mill.

THE ROMAN BRIDGE. In the early 1900s this was the most photographed place in the area: with people, without people, in summer and in winter, from both sides near and far! Not Roman, but an old pack horse bridge, it was renamed to attract tourists.

THE ROMAN LAKES, EARLY 1900s. Rowing boats were available for hire. The tea rooms and lakes were entered by turnstiles, one of which can be seen on the left hand side. These photographs of the Roman Lakes area, which is on the other side of the River Goyt from the Strines Road, are in Mellor, but are inevitably referred to as being in Marple!

Three
Marple Centre and Brabyns Brow

MARKET STREET, *c.* 1968.

STOCKPORT ROAD, 1997. No mill dominates the street today. (See page 18) Traffic lights, street furniture and road markings show the impact of the car and the lorry.

CHURCH LANE. Not much has changed here today since this was taken in the early 1900s except for the new windows, in many different sztyles from the originals. The old cottages that used to be next to the Jolly Sailor can be seen at the end of the road.

CHURCH LANE. This shows the start of the demolition of houses in the late 1960s to make space for the extension of Hibbert Lane to Stockport Road. Houses were also pulled down at the Stockport end of the new road. Other buildings, including Walsh's building yard, were removed to make way for the thoroughfare.

CHADWICK STREET. This view shows more buildings that did not survive the alterations of the late sixties and early seventies. Many terraced houses were demolished to make the car park behind Market Street. In the centre of the photograph is the hall that was built for use as a Girl's Institute. (See page 80) It was bought by All Saints' Church in 1935 for £947 for use as a parish hall. During the Second World War it functioned as a British Restaurant. Workmen can be seen dismantling the roof of the house next to the hall.

CHURCH LANE AND CHADWICK STREET. The top of the ridge of the Methodist Church can just be seen over the roof of the cottage in this view from the early 1900s. In the distance on the right is the Conservative Club.

MARKET STREET, c. 1910. This view looks down Market Street from Church Lane. What a pity the canopy over the pavement from the shops, built in 1908, no longer exists. Also demolished are Trinity Primitive Chapel, the second Co-op and Hollins Mill chimney, all to be seen at the far end of the street. The road was pedestrianised in the early 1970s.

WHIT WALK, MARKET STREET, EARLY 1900s. Some of the cottages have their original steps up to living floors and down to cellars. The one on the right still has its small paned window. The Bull's Head hotel can be seen in the middle distance with the very old Linn Row cottages alongside. They were reputed to have been lived in by linen weavers, hence their name.

DERBY WAY. Just before pedestrianisation in the early 1970s, this view, looks from Market Street towards Walsh's builders yard, which is now a car park. (See page 33) There were ambitious plans for the complete development of the centre of Marple, but the developers went bankrupt and Marple Council had a rethink on a more modest scale.

STOCKPORT ROAD, LATE 1960s. The buildings remain. The Dolce Vita restaurant is now operating in John William's shop; his delivery van can be seen parked at the roadside. It was used as a launderette for many years. The Copper Kettle is now a Chinese takeaway.

UNION ROOMS, STOCKPORT ROAD, 1895. The Union Rooms were built in 1878 by Thomas Carver, one of the owners of Hollins Mill, as a coffee tavern and mission hall for the people of Marple. This was as an alternative to the numerous public houses of the district. For many years it has been the Regent Cinema. Marple is one of very few small towns to still have its own picture house. Just beyond the rooms are the lodge and entrance to the drive that led to Carver's home, Hollins House, which is now the council offices. (See page 108)

CANAL BUILDINGS, EARLY 1900s. Most of the terrace on the left is still there, just off the Stockport Road, next to the Navigation Inn. The stone built row on the right was constructed by Samuel Oldknow. They were demolished in 1957. So many of the buildings that have been pulled down, even relatively recently, would be saved today! Modernised, they would now be 'very desirable'.

VIEW FROM TOP LOCK, 1950s. The large, low building on the left of the picture was originally Jink's Tea Rooms. The site is just above the lime kilns and when the kilns were working, the boats would have unloaded their lime and coal straight into the top of the furnaces. (See page 114) The kilns were closed in the late 1890s and the tea room was built to cater for the thousands of trippers who visited the area in the first half of this century.

PUBLIC LAVATORIES, OLDKNOW RECREATION GROUND, 1995. Now closed, these lavatories were constructed with some of the stone from Marple Hall, demolished in 1959. The toilets on Mellor Recreation Ground, also closed - some of the retaining walls on Cross Lane, Brabyns Brow and by the Ring of Bells, are constructed of the same honey coloured stone. (See page 12)

BRICK ROW, c. 1900. This long row of cottages built of brick was erected by Samuel Oldknow for his workers. The houses were demolished soon after the photograph was taken to make way for the new Arkwright Road.

STONE ROW. Viewed in the early 1900s, Stone Row, at the top of the road leading down to the Roman Lakes from the Oldknow Recreation Ground, was demolished, despite efforts to save it, in 1936. The row was built by Samuel Oldknow for his workers in 1794. The building on the left was meant be a market hall but Stockport refused permission, so it was adapted as more homes. In 1891, just before the mill burnt down, there were 110 adults and children living there in thirty-one houses. Another five were empty. The houses were back to backs. (See page 109)

HOLLINS LANE, 1989. The demolition of the remaining parts of Hollins Mill, which had been used by different firms since its closure in the 1950s. A new supermarket was being erected on the site, the frame of which can be seen in the photograph.

STATION ROAD. Seen here in the early 1900s, Station Road, looks much wider than it really is, even now. The cottages on the right had the date stone 1791, which predates the turnpiking of the road in 1802. They were demolished in the 1970s and replaced by flats for senior citizens.

BRABYNS BROW, *c.* 1955. A man can be seen emerging from the entrance of the station yard, complete with its fancy lamp. The Brow used to have more mature beech trees and people complained about the droppings from the rookery! The elm trees that edged the Memorial Park higher up the road had to be felled in the 1970s because they were dying of Dutch Elm disease.

BRABYNS HALL, LOWER MARPLE, EARLY 1900s. Brabyns Hall was demolished in 1952. It stood on the site of the present car park and now only the grounds remain as a recreation area. The original farmhouse was incorporated into a new building in 1750 by Dr Henry Brabyn, hence its name. It was the Hudson family, later owners of the estate, who gave the land and most of the money to build St Martin's Church, Vicarage and School. The last owner, Miss Fanny Hudson, inherited the hall in 1906 and lived there until her death in 1941. (See page 89)

MARPLE BRIDGE. This view looks across the bridge in the early 1900s from the Derbyshire side of the River Goyt towards Brabyns Brow, before its widening in 1930. The steepness of the hill and dangerous bend to the right around Dr Hibbert's house, seen in the centre of the picture, plus the inadequate brakes of vehicles, led to an increasing number of accidents. (See page 69) When the bridge was widened the two cottages next to it were demolished, and the new line of the road was distanced from the remaining houses, giving them front gardens. Dr Hibbert's house was removed at this time. The cottages behind the Midland Hotel have gone since the photograph was taken but the pub, extended and modernised, is still there.

Four
Ludworth and
Marple Bridge

CORNER OF COMPSTALL ROAD AND GLOSSOP ROAD, *c.* 1905.

THE HORSE SHOE INN. Shown here in the early 1900s, the inn, that used to be where the Horse Shoe Garage is now, was demolished when Marple Bridge was widened in 1930. Its removal also allowed the straightening of the sharp bend into Lower Fold. Behind the inn can be seen the Co-op store, complete with a sign advertising teas. On the opposite side of the road are the stables and yard of the Norfolk Arms. They have since disappeared to be replaced by a car park.

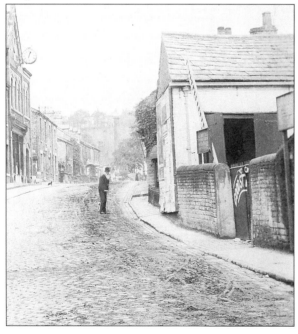

MARPLE BRIDGE GAS WORKS. The detail of the end of Lower Fold from the previous photograph shows the chimney of the gas works. The houses on the Glossop Road can just be seen. (See page 114)

PEAR TREE FARM, LOWER FOLD. James Samuel Arden (1854-1922) and his wife Mary Ann Fielding (1856-1945), are seen here in the early 1900s, in the yard of the farm. With them are their children, Clara, Elizabeth, Frank, William, Samuel, James, Mary and Charles. One son is missing from the photograph.

HEYS FARM. On the other side of Lower Fold to Pear Tree Farm were the fields of Heys Farm. The family and their horses are dressed for a carnival parade in the early 1900s. Behind the horses is the site of the Ludworth and Mellor Women's Institute Hall, that was built in 1926.

HEYS FARMHOUSE, EARLY 1900s. The farmhouse was demolished when the Bonnington Estate was built on the farm land in the 1970s.

ROSE BROW. Known today as Compstall Road, the scene has changed very little since the photograph was taken in the early 1900s. The galleries of a large coal mine extended underground from the Glossop Road down to the River Etherow. The mine, which was entered down Coal Pit Lane, was working by 1840 and closed in the 1880s. It belonged to the Jowett family who owned a large estate in Mellor (See page 55). Coal was mined all over the area and in the last century around ten per cent of the working population were miners.

WEEKEND COTTAGE, SANDHILL LANE, 1930s. During the twenties and thirties many 'shacks' were erected in Ludworth as weekend homes. They had names such as Jazz King, The Plaza, Stirrup Have and Blue Heaven. Many tales were told of the 'going ons' up on Ludworth Moor! Nearly all were demolished in the late fifties.

LANE ENDS, GLOSSOP ROAD, *c.* 1920. There cannot be a great deal of traffic on the road as the North Western bus has stopped right in the centre of it. On the left is the Lane Ends and on the right is the Travellers Call.

PEAR TREE FARM, MILL BROW, 1960s. The old farm and its outbuildings were renovated and modernised in the 1960s, but the old windows and beams have been kept. It is a late sixteenth century building incorporating parts of the earlier timber framed house. There are two cruck built barns, in one of which the Congregationalists first worshipped in the 1660s. (See pages 27 and 50)

MOUNT ST JOSEPH'S CONVENT. The convent, seen here in the early 1900s, was erected in the first two years of this century. It was a small boarding school and laundry run as part of a larger community in Salford. In summer it was used for holidays and outings for the sisters and children from the city. It closed in 1932 and was used for a time as a poultry farm. Later it became a guest house and restaurant. It was demolished in the early seventies and houses were erected on the site.

ST MARY'S, HOLLINS LANE, EARLY 1900s. Roman Catholics first met for worship in cottages in Ludworth in the 1830s. The Duke of Norfolk, Lord of the Manor of Glossop and a prominent Catholic, gave land and money to build the church. Many Irish moved into the area with the building of the railway in the early 1860s. Most moved on, but quite a number of families settled in Marple Bridge, establishing an Irish community in the area at the end of the last century.

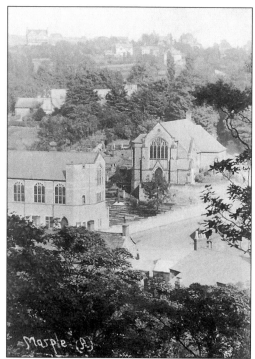

CONGREGATIONAL CHURCH AND SUNDAY SCHOOL, 1910s. At the corner of Town Street and Hollins Lane, the building on the left is the Sunday School of the Congregational Church shortly after its completion in 1907. On the first floor was a large hall, complete with a stage. It was erected on the site of the their second chapel, built in 1789. The first chapel was in Mill Brow, and was built after their first services were held in a cruck barn. In 1887 the third church was built just up Hollins Lane. The Sunday School was sold in the 1970s and is now used by doctors and dentists for their surgeries. (See page 48)

OLD TOLL HOUSE, MARPLE BRIDGE, 1890s. The building was used as a shop at the time of the photograph. It was built as a toll house on the Marple Bridge to Hayfield Turnpike in 1792. The traffic would have included a large number of carts going to and from the cotton mills in Mellor. It was demolished in 1923; the site of the toll house and the cottages behind it is now the car park at the bottom of Hollins Lane.

TOWN STREET, EARLY 1900s. Just who are the well hatted people walking in the middle of the street? Perhaps it was Sunday morning and they had just attended the Congregational Chapel. The old frontage of the Railway public house, now called the Royal Scot, can be seen behind the strollers.

TOWN STREET. The buildings remain but the street scene has altered considerably since this view in the early 1900s. The old river wall, which collapsed in December 1991, can be clearly seen. (See page 74) The vehicle into which a lady is climbing is the first bus that ran to Mellor. The service was started by Joe Hinchcliffe after the First World War using an ex-army flat based lorry onto which he built the cover. The passengers sat facing each other on two wooden benches - a very rough ride!

SKATING ON THE RIVER GOYT IN THE EARLY 1900s. There were several hard winters at the start of this century and skating was possible on the mill pond of the corn mill. It was situated behind the Midland and was erected in 1691; it was most likely the site of the earlier manorial mill of the Bradshaws of Marple Hall. It ceased working in the 1930s and was later demolished. The weir was lowered in the 1960s to try and relieve the problem of foam blowing off the polluted river into Town Street.

TOWN STREET, c. 1932. After the widening of the bridge and the straightening of the road in 1930, the cottages on the left now have gardens. The Norfolk Arms still has its adjoining stables and cottages. At the top of the hill can be seen the convent on Hollins Lane. Where there are fields, St Mary's School and the Constable Estate are now situated.

Five

Mellor

INTERIOR OF NEW HOUSE HILL METHODIST CHAPEL, EARLY 1900s.

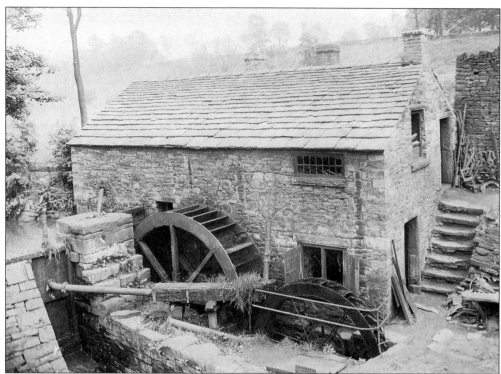

SPADE FORGE. Compare this photograph from the early 1900s with the modern one below. Once used to make spades and shovels with a water-powered tilt hammer, the building has undergone many changes of use and alterations to the fabric. During the 1980s the wheel was restored and in 1996 it was substantially reconstructed and extended for use as a home.

Mellor Road and Townscliffe Lane, Marple Bridge.

LONGHURST LANE, *c.* 1915. Known as Mellor Road in the early years of this century, perhaps the inhabitants of the new Edwardian villas did not think the old name smart enough and changed it. The old gate posts that used to stand at the end of Townscliffe Lane have been removed, and the start of the new Clement Road can just be seen on the left.

CATARACT BRIDGE, LONGHURST LANE, 1911. The curve in the road has been somewhat straightened but it still remains dangerous for the speeding motorist. Cataract Mill, just to be seen on the right, built around 1890 for the manufacture of cotton wool and wadding, was owned by the Jowett family. The firm had warehouses in Manchester, Leeds, Birmingham and Dublin. This is the only mill in the district still in production. (See page 47)

ROYAL OAK, LONGHURST LANE. On the left can be seen the Mellor branch of the Compstall Co-op, opened in 1918, so this photograph from the early part of the century must have been taken after that date. The Co-op closed in the 1960s. (See page 96) Behind the Royal Oak in the 1850s was a small brick and tile works employing three brickmakers and two tile carriers.

DAMSTEADS, 1930s. Built as hand-loom weavers' cottages, the outside steps that led to the third-storey working loft can clearly be seen. Mellor had boom years in the late eighteenth and early nineteenth centuries when there was a glut of yarn from the new spinning mills and no factory-powered looms. Damsteads Cotton Mills used to be situated in the valley behind the houses. One of the mills went up in flames in the early 1860s. The house was modernised and substantially extended in the 1980s.

APPLE TREE FARM AND LONGHURST LANE. This is the view down the lane in the early 1900s before any of the ribbon development. The barn attached to the farm is now a house. Apple Tree Cottage, seen just behind the cow, was demolished and a large bungalow was erected on the site further back from the road.

MELLOR RECREATION GROUND, 1960s. In the name of safety, all the playground equipment seen in the photograph has gone! A few new pieces have been placed in the far corner of the field. The toilets, now closed, were built in 1959 from the stone of the demolished Marple Hall. The field was the site of the Mellor Cricket Club. (See page 82)

DEVONSHIRE ARMS, 1935. The public house is hung with bunting to celebrate the Jubilee of George V. The milk in churns from the nearby farms is ready for collection by George Brough to take to Marple Station. How many of today's children know what a milk churn was? The telephone box is by the wall where an old style one remains today. The bus time table would have shown the times of many more buses than there are today, including some in the evenings and on Sunday.

TARDEN COTTAGES, GIBB LANE, EARLY 1900s. The cottage in the middle distance was the first place for the Cathedral Home. (See page 92)

MELLOR CHURCH. Seen here in the early 1900s, a church has stood on this hill for many hundreds of years. The oldest parts to survive are bits of the tower with its fifteenth century window and an even more ancient door. The chancel and nave were rebuilt at the start of the last century. For many years there were three galleries, and when the last gallery was removed in the first years of this century, the two tiers of windows were replaced by a row of single ones. The church remains in the Diocese of Derby, Mellor's only remaining link with its old county after it was 'moved' to Cheshire in 1936.

INTERIOR OF MELLOR CHURCH, c. 1920s. The pulpit is carved out of the trunk of an oak tree and is believed to be the oldest in Britain, if not Europe. It narrowly escaped destruction in the last century when it lay unused in the tower and the gravedigger was told to chop it up! It proved too hard a job so he used it as a storage place for his tools! It was reinstated towards the end of the century.

OLD VICARAGE, *c.* 1900. The Reverend Thomas M. Freeman stands at the front of his garden and house. Originally the Church Inn, it was bought by his maternal grandfather in 1782. When Thomas, the last of three generations of vicars died in 1906, the church thought the house was theirs and asked his widow to leave. She produced the deeds proving ownership and the church then purchased the house that had been the second Church Inn as a new vicarage.

MELLOR HALL, *c.* 1920s. The only remaining hall in the area, there has been a house on the site from medieval times and the present building dates from the late 1600s.

MELLOR'S WATER SUPPLY, 1925. Despite the sewering of the road from Moor End to Marple Bridge in the early years of this century, Mellor's expansion was held up by the lack of a good water supply. After twenty years of debate water was brought from the lower slopes of Kinder Scout. This photograph shows the water being turned on in Brook Bottom.

NEW HOUSE HILL METHODIST CHAPEL, 1930s. The Sunday School anniversary included a walk through the village with stops to sing hymns, followed by services and a tea in the chapel. The building had mostly been built with money given by Thomas Waller, who was one of the owners of the big Dove Bank Mill in Moor End. His was the only tombstone in front of the chapel; it remains today despite the conversion of the chapel into a house.

CHEETHAM HILL LADS' HOLIDAY HOME. There were several holiday homes for children and adults in Mellor. The area was seen as a healthy and invigorating place for the people of the nearby overcrowded and polluted industrial towns. Seen here in the early 1900s are thirteen boys looking at the photographer, so they must have quite tightly packed into the cottage!

ROBIN HOOD'S PICKING RODS. This photograph was taken in the early 1900s on one of the occasions when the stones were vandalised, not a new phenomenon! Also known as the Maiden Stones, no one is sure of their origin, but they are certainly nothing to do with Robin Hood. The most likely explanation is that they are marking stones as they stand at the junction of Mellor, Ludworth and Chisworth.

Six

Events

PROCESSION OF LOCAL DIGNITARIES TO ALL SAINTS' CHURCH, *c.* 1905.

CORONATION CELEBRATIONS, MELLOR, 1911. This is one of a series of postcards produced commemorating the celebrations for the coronation of George V. The procession finished with races and tea in the Mellor sports grounds. The whole population of the village seems to have turned out for the occasion.

CORONATION DECORATIONS, MARPLE, 1911. Stockport Road was decorated with bunting for the occasion. The building on the right, at the end of Market Street, had replaced an earlier one and was used by Vernons the furnisher and undertaker. The building was later used by Marple Urban District Council for its offices.

FUND RAISING, FIRST WORLD WAR. At Christmas in 1914, the window of the council offices on Market Street was filled with cards noting donations given 'to send a seasonable present to every one of the gallant men of our village who have responded to the call of their King and Country. Marple has done nobly by already sending about 150 men to join the colours'.

CELEBRATING THE END OF THE WAR, 1918. The enormous bonfire was built on the Ridge and when lit, it must have been visible for miles around.

FOUNDATION STONE LAYING, 1906. At the laying of the foundation stone for a new social club at Hawk Green, the local newspaper reported 'Amid great rejoicing the foundation stones of the new building were laid in the presence of a large crowd of spectators. Mr W. Bradbury JP, Chairman of the Urban District Council presided... man was made a social animal and yearned to meet with his fellow men... no politics or sectarianism were to be allowed'.

THE START OF GOYT MILL, 20 JULY 1905. The local newspaper reported that Councillor Pearson, who cut the first sod, said 'he hoped the shareholders of the new mill would receive good dividends at all times. The directors hoped to find employment for something like 300 hands... that £450 to £500 would be paid in wages to the village'.

CONCERT IN RIDGE QUARRY, 1909. During the first decade of this century many events took place in the old quarry, especially concerts for organisations wishing to raise money. The band in this picture can be seen in a circle on the left.

ST MARY'S DRUMMER BOYS, JUNE 1909. The boys were taking part in the Compstall Carnival. (See page 49)

WALKING RACE, APRIL 1904. This photograph shows the race nearing its end in Stockport Road. The local paper reported 'When nearing Marple a grand struggle took place between Heastie and Rimmer but the Staffordshire man managed to make a supreme effort at the close and won the cup, although there was only a few seconds between the pair'.

ROSE QUEEN CELEBRATIONS, 1949. Marple Congregational Church, along with many others, had an annual Rose Queen and attendants. The change over was marked by a procession and a crowning. Here the Sunday School banners are clearly visible.

ACCIDENT ON BRABYNS BROW, 1920s. This was just one of the many accidents that happened before Brabyns Brow was straightened and Marple Bridge widened. The coal lorry ended up inside the house! The photographer, Mr Garner, had his studio on Lower Fold and must have arrived quickly on the scene with his camera. The new postcard would probably have been ready for sale by the next day. (See page 42)

ACCIDENT IN COMPSTALL, 1903. At the bottom of Compstall Brow, another vehicle has lost control. The mill can be seen on the left and the Athenaeum, at present the library, is behind the cottages. This was built by the Andrews family, the mill owners, for their employees to use for recreation and education. Many of the residents of Ludworth worked in the mill.

ACCIDENT, HOLLINS LANE, MARPLE BRIDGE. In October 1970, Police Constable Mike Kelly and another person look at an overturned car. Luckily its driver was unhurt.

FLOODS AT MOOR END, 1967. A violent thunderstorm produced these floods which washed a hole in the road. In the first years of the last century there was a mill pond on the left of the road. The water was used to power the wheels of William Radcliffe's cotton mills that were in the hollow on the other side of the road. During the floods the culvert must have been blocked, causing the destruction of the road surface.

SPEECHES IN THE MEMORIAL PARK, *c.* 1920. The event is unknown, but the clergy were involved so it may not have been political. Perhaps it was to raise money for the war memorial? In the background is Hollins House, bought by Marple Council from the Carver family in the 1920s. It is still used as Stockport Council's area offices.

THANK YOU MR HODGKINSON, *c.* 1910. Another unknown event which took place inside Hollins Mill; the building was decorated for the occasion. Perhaps he had given them a Christmas party?

MELLOR HERITAGE EXHIBITION, MAY 1984. The history of the village was told inside the church. The event attracted crowds of people.

OLDKNOW 200, 1990. To celebrate the bicentenary of the laying of the foundation stone of Samuel Oldknow's Mellor Mill, two weeks of events were held. These included a play about his life which was performed in the open air, concerts, the carnival and an exhibition held in the library. The children in the photograph had dressed as apprentices and were visiting Bottoms Hall, where they would have lived in the early 1800s.

COLLAPSE OF RIVER WALL, MARPLE BRIDGE, 1991. Part of the wall collapsed into the river during the night of 21 December, taking the gas pipe with it. Town Street was closed for a year during the building of the new wall. The construction work provided much interest to the onlookers. The opportunity was taken to provide new pavements on both sides of the road and Victorian style street furniture.

CELEBRATIONS FOR NEW WALL. These took the form of a street party in December 1992 for the reopening of Town Street. The road was opened by Mellor Church Rose Queen, and a fire engine from Marple was the first vehicle to travel along it. The Marple Choir sang carols and everyone was extremely relieved, especially those traders still in business, that the whole project was completed.

Seven

People

MARPLE'S POLICE FORCE, *c.* 1925.

JUDGE BRADSHAW, 1650s. Marple's most famous son, Judge Bradshaw was the brother of Henry, the builder of Marple Hall. A staunch Puritan and a lawyer, he became the President of the Council that tried Charles I for treason. His is the first signature on the king's death warrant. He died just before the restoration of the monarchy and was buried in Westminster Abbey. Charles II had the bodies of Cromwell and Bradshaw exhumed, taken through the streets of London and hung at Tyburn. Their heads were then set on posts outside Westminster Hall. (See page 12)

RICHARD AND CHRISTOPHER ISHERWOOD, c. 1912. They were the nephews of Henry, who died, childless, in 1940. Christopher, the elder, gave the estate to his brother. He became a novelist, left England in 1939 and spent the rest of his life in Hollywood. He wrote the book *Goodbye to Berlin* that was later made into the film *Cabaret*. Richard lived at Wybersley Hall, the other home of the family, and Marple Hall was allowed to fall into ruin. Neither brother married.

ALL SAINTS' SCHOOL. The Violets Drill Group are practising in September 1924. On the back of the card are the following names: Elsie Woodcock, Eva Frost, Edith Eastwood, Miriam Brook, Ann Kershaw, Marion Goddard, Hilda Lee, Mary Waterhouse, Margaret Hudson and Eileen Doughty. Unfortunately only ten names are given so one is missing, and which name matches which girl?

ALBERT SCHOOLS, EARLY 1900s. Started as a Sunday School for the Congregational Church on Hibbert Lane, it also became a day school in 1868. The Carvers and Hodgkinsons, who owned and ran Hollins Mill, were strong supporters of the church and school. Attendance at this school instead of All Saints was said to help you get work in the mill!

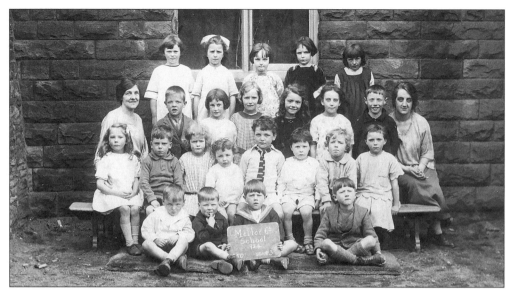

MELLOR SCHOOL, 1924. Unfortunately just a few names are known. Back row, left to right: Betty Sigley, -?-, Nellie Nadin, ? Davies. Middle Row: Mrs Bartlett (headmistress) and at the other end of the row, Miss Jeffs. Mellor School started life in 1639 in a small building in the churchyard. The photograph is taken outside the third school, which was built below the church in 1880.

LUDWORTH SCHOOL, 1931. Back row, from left to right: ? Wood, Arthur Hickman, Ronnie Whitehead, Frank Hart, Maurice Oglam, Ronnie Booth. Third row: Eileen Osbeliston, -?-, Nancy Hill, Eileen Shallcross, Hessie Gobson, Eileen Grimshaw, Irene Potts. Second row: Mr Butterworth (headmaster), Marjorie Jenkins, Stanley Young, Phyllis Knowles, Alan Gerrard, Freda Hughes, Sam Porter, D. Lees, Miss Ardern. Front row: Marjorie Coulam, Geoff Henry, May Heath, Margaret Sigley, Flora Sidebottom, Gwennie Harrop. The school was built in 1907.

THE 1st MARPLE GIRL GUIDES COMPANY, *c.* 1920

MARPLE SCOUTS, *c.* 1916. The *High Peak Reporter* newspaper recorded in April 1908, that 'A troop of Baden Powell Boy Scouts is to be established at Marple and it is expected that Miss Freda Barlow of Woodville will be the Scoutmaster. We wish the project every success and that all the Marple mothers will encourage their boys to become members, for a genuine BP Scout is a gentleman whether he be rich or poor'.

CONGREGATIONAL BOYS BRIGADE, *c.* 1910. These boys of the Marple Bridge Chapel Brigade have lined up smartly for the photographer. Only the surname of the leader is known - Higgenbotham.

MARPLE GIRLS' CLUB UNION, MAY 1912 The shield on the right is a 'prize for plain sewing'!

LUDWORTH LADIES' HOCKEY TEAM, *c.* 1910. The names on the back of the card are: Miss Anderson, Miss Newton, Miss Parkinson, Miss Hope, Miss Rimmer, R. Sinclair, M. McLaine, K. Wilson, ? Humphrey, E. Scholes, E. Evans, B. Lillie.

MARPLE CONGREGATIONAL CHURCH FOOTBALL TEAM. Photographed in the spring of 1908, they are the proud winners of the Stockport Cup for the season 1907/8. Goalkeeper: J. Pollard. Backs: S. Graham, F. Goodwin, S. Porter, J. Wilde. Forwards: ? Bates, ? Arderne, T. Moss, N. Austin, ? Barnett, ? Bradbury. Trainer: O. Graham.

MELLOR CRICKET CLUB. The cricket pitch and the pavilion no longer exist. The pitch is now part of the Mellor Recreation Ground, situated on the side of Longhurst Lane below Church Road. (See page 57)

WATCHING THE MATCH, 1930s. The spectators have all looked round for the photographer; the pavilion is in the background. In the early 1930s the club closed when the new owner of Mellor Hall tried to get permission to build houses on the land. His application was refused; the council then bought the land and turned it into a recreation ground.

MELLOR LACROSSE FIRST TEAM, 1928-29. The history of the club, published for its fiftieth anniversary, records that 'The winning of this Championship (Third Division) was marked with a great show of enthusiasm. Lacrosse had by now become firmly established in Mellor and the Lacrosse Club was one of the institutions of the village'. Back row, left to right: J. Jowett, W. Wilson, J. Turner, W. Fairbank, T. Oldham, C. Middleton. Front row: W. Templeton, C. Templeton, N. Bennett, H. Oldham, K. Smith, G. Johnson. Lacrosse is still played in Mellor today.

MARPLE REED BAND, *c.* 1905. On 4 September 1900, at a meeting held in Trinity Hall, Market Street, it was decided to form a reed band. Their first recorded engagement was for the Marple Flower Show and Sports in the following year. Over the years they have had times of success and difficulty. Last year they won the Gold Challenge Trophy and £2,500 at the British Open Band Championships. Their principal cornet player, Helen Fox, was awarded the individual championship prize. The *Guardian* newspaper included in its half page report of the event that 'the Marple Band from Cheshire, a penniless minnow, had been drawn to play last... Marple is broke. It came by train because it could not afford to hire a bus'! Despite all that, they were the top band.

RIDGE METHODISTS BAND OF HOPE OUTING, 1909. Judging by the number of people at the outing to Alderley Edge, the organisation was thriving. Band of Hope members were pledged to total abstinence from alcohol. (See page 23)

NURSE WALKER, JULY 1910. When Nurse Walker resigned from the Marple Bridge Sick Nursing Society, the local paper reported, 'The Revd Hickson presented on behalf of the committee and subscribers a neat silver tea service as a parting and marriage gift. Reference was made to Miss Walker's long and useful service in the district'. The photograph was taken on Low Lea Road with Town Street in the background.

JOHN HADFIELD AND THE FARM WORKERS, EARLY 1900s. They worked the Mellor Hall Farm of which the barn, with the date of construction of 1686, still exists. It has in recent years been converted into a home and the raised walkway is no longer there.

GEORGE WHEELDON, EARLY 1900s. George farmed land close by his shop on St Martin's Road, previously known as Wharf Road. Some of his land later became the Oldknow Recreation Ground. (See page 103)

MARPLE CATTLE MARKET, 1930s. The market was opened in 1909 and closed in the 1960s. Market day was Monday, when the public houses in Marple Bridge were allowed to be open all day! Just imagine the chaos that would be created now if cattle were driven up Brabyns Brow! In 1920, newly calved cows fetched £50 each.

HOLLINS GREEN FARM. This picture from the early 1900s shows threshing, using a steam engine for power. The farm stood just off Hollins Lane, opposite the fire station. The site is now occupied by two pairs of modern semi-detached houses. There are very few photographs of farming in Marple, although most of the land remained in agricultural use until the building boom of the 1960s.

COMPSTALL MILL WEAVERS, c. 1900s. The picture, taken in the yard of the mill, includes what seem to us today some very young children. They would have been part timers, working either in the mill mornings or afternoons and attending school for the rest of the time. They often fell asleep over their desks and were beaten by the teacher for it.

HAWK GREEN MILL GIRL, EARLY 1900s.

SOLDIERS AT BRABYNS HALL. During the First World War the hall was used as a convalescent home for wounded servicemen. In the centre of the picture is Miss Hudson, the owner, and her companion. (See page 41) A local paper reported in September 1914: 'Brabyns Hall has now been got ready... for the reception of wounded and invalid soldiers and sailors. The public can view the Hall on payment of 2d each which goes towards Red Cross Funds'.

PERCY MARSLAND AND FRIENDS. This photograph was taken in France during the First World War when they were relaxing from the fierce fighting in the trenches. Percy, from Mellor, in the centre of the back row, survived the war and lived until the 1980s.

PETER ARNFIELD, *c.* 1890s. He was coachman and gardener at one of the big houses on the Glossop Road.

WEDDING PARTY, *c.* 1918. Seen here are Sarah Elizabeth Arden and Harry Lockwood after their marriage, together with guests outside No.26 Lower Fold, Marple Bridge. (See page 103)

TWO SMART YOUNG MEN. The date is unknown, but the man on the left is Frank Barrow.

THE OLD FIDDLER OF SLACK WOOD. His name was Thomas Chetham and he was buried in the churchyard at Mellor in September 1906; this picture was taken in the very early years of the century. Born in 1819, he was reputed to be a veteran of the Crimean War. Model wooden soldiers can be seen above his head. The house was demolished and rebuilt after his death.

VISITORS TO THE CATHEDRAL HOME. This photograph, taken in the early 1900s, was taken outside Primrose Cottage, Tarden, Mellor. The holiday home, started by people from Manchester Cathedral, began its life in the cottage in 1890 and moved to a purpose built home on Longhurst Lane in 1907.

SCHOOL ROW, MELLOR, 1911. The old gentleman standing at the gate of his cottage was probably waiting for, or had just seen, the procession in Mellor to celebrate the coronation of George V.

TEA PARTY ON HOLLINS LANE, *c.* 1900. Tea is being taken on the lawn of the Oakes of Hollins Lane, Marple Bridge. The family were the Radcliffes, who owned the cotton mill in Holly Vale. The mill was situated on the other side of the stream below the Hare and Hounds in Mill Brow.

THE TOILERS, *c.* 1900. Rather a contrast to the photograph above! A local photographer took the picture, which is believed to be of the workers making the tunnel for the Hazel Grove to Chinley railway, near Wybersley.

LAST MEETING OF MARPLE URBAN DISTRICT COUNCIL. In 1974 Marple became part of Stockport Metropolitan Borough Council in the newly created county of Greater Manchester. Standing, from the right: Alex Finnie, ? Burns, ? Carter, Jack Brady, ? Chronnell, Harvey Cooke, ? Turner (clerk to council), Paul Hickey (chairman), ? Lomas, Gerald Tracy (vice chairman), ? Ball (surveyor), Jim Headridge, ? Hunter (deputy surveyor), Monty Burton, ? Mason, ? Yarwood, ? Boardman. Seated, from right: Ann Clarke, Joy Hearle, Peter Reed, Ted Sandal, ? Haseltine.

Eight

Shops

SHAW'S BUTCHERS SHOP, FORGE BANK, MELLOR, EARLY 1900s.

THE ORIGINAL COMPSTALL CO-OP SHOP, EARLY 1900s. The Compstall Co-operative and Industrial Society was formed in 1851, with the backing of the Andrews, the local mill owners. The first shop was in a building on Compstall Road that stands just before the George Hotel and the bridge over the River Etherow. It proved such a success that other shops were opened in the district. The society eventually had branches in Marple, Marple Bridge, High Lane, Rose Hill, Romiley and Mellor. There were drapery stores, a bakery, shoe menders, coal yards and delivery vehicles, amongst others. There was even a hall in Marple Bridge for social events and it was there that the famous dividend was collected for many years.

from "The Wheatsheaf" September, 1935

YOURS!

Do you realise that
COMPSTALL CO-OPERATIVE
SOCIETY *has*

Grocery Shops

Drapery Shops

Butchery Shops

Fish Shop

Confectionery Departments

Tailoring Departments

Coal Department

Dairy Service

Boot and Shoe Repairing Service

Laundry Service

Funeral Furnishing Service

Optical Service

Banking Service

Building Society Agency

National Health Insurance
    Agency

One Travelling Grocers' Shop

One Travelling Butchers' Shop

Two Travelling Bread Vans

One Travelling Fish Cart, and

A Collective Life Assurance
    Scheme which covers every
    Member ?

All this is yours

Take Advantage of it

ADVERTISEMENT FOR THE CO-OP, 1930s. Just look at the great number of goods and services that the society provided.

THE FIRST CO-OP SHOP IN MARPLE, *c.* 1901. The Marple branch was opened in 1874 because people did not want to walk all the way to Compstall. An existing shop was taken over and it was an immediate success.

THE SECOND MARPLE CO-OP, *c.* 1915. A new purpose built shop on the same site was opened in 1913 and was also a great success. This shop, with its wooden counters and staff serving the customers every product from the shelves, closed in 1976.

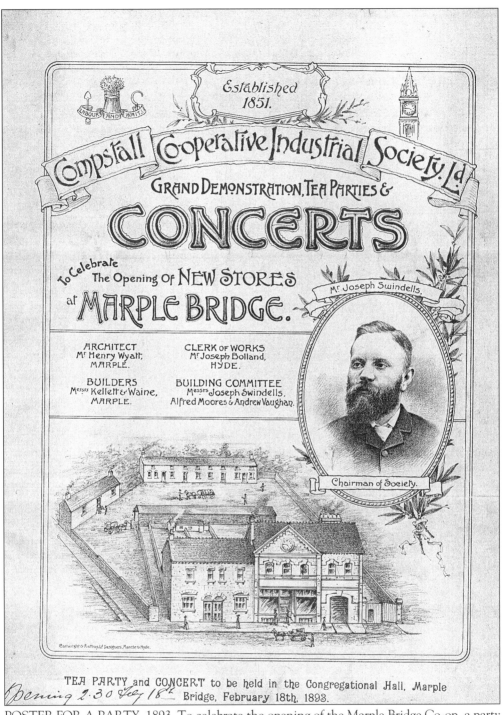

POSTER FOR A PARTY, 1893. To celebrate the opening of the Marple Bridge Co-op, a party was held in Marple. The buildings included offices, stables, and the bakery and it became the business centre of the society. The store closed in 1973. In the autumn of 1996 the stables were demolished and new houses have been erected on the site.

MARPLE CO-OP SHOPS, 1960s. Situated at the corner of Stockport Road and Market Street is the furnishing department, with the second grocery store behind it. Trinity Methodist Church can be seen on the far right. A third Co-op was erected on the site in 1976. This time it was a supermarket. This shop was closed when an even bigger store was built on the site of Hollins Mill, on the other side of the Stockport Road in 1989.

HAWK GREEN CO-OP, c. 1901. The shop was sited on the corner of Upper Hibbert Lane and Barnsfold Road. The store in the photograph was opened in 1892, succeeding an earlier one on the opposite side of the road that had been there for ten years.

BUTCHERS SHOP, 1912. The shop of Arthur Joseph Hawley, pork butcher, stood at No.60 Market Street. He had previously traded from a shop at No.94 Church Lane, and then at No.41 Market Street.

ARDERN'S OF TOWN STREET, MARPLE BRIDGE. Just look at all the meat hanging outside the shop, well within biting distance of the dog, in this picture from the early 1900s! The meat would also have been covered with flies and the dust of passing traffic just a few feet away. Nearly all game and meat shops hung their goods outside.

HART'S OF MARPLE BRIDGE, EARLY 1900s. This wholesale and retail poultry shop was at the Mellor end of Town Street, facing the road. A fine range of birds hangs outside the shop, complete with heads, wings and feet.

FISH AND CHIP SHOP AT No.103 CHURCH LANE, 1935. It could be that this was the same man that had the butchers on Market Street because the photograph has written on the back 'A. Hawley standing at the door of his shop'.

While in Marple call at
Higgins' Tea Rooms

70, STOCKPORT ROAD,

(Opposite Marple Post Office)

Buses from Stockport pass the door.

7 mins. walk from Rose Hill and 10 mins. from Marple
Station.

SWEETS, ICES, MINERALS &
TOBACCO.

NUMBER 70 STOCKPORT ROAD, 1930s. The Marple Book Shop now occupies the premises.

BEECH HOUSE, *c.* 1905. George Wheeldon's grocery and provision shop was situated on the corner of Oldknow and St Martins Roads. Previously he had had a shop in nearby Brick Row. (See page 38) The shop was unchanged until it closed in the late sixties. It was then a beauty parlour and has now been converted into a home for the elderly. (See page 86)

LOWER FOLD, MARPLE BRIDGE. Number 19 was the home of Mr Ardern, a cabinet maker and french polisher. (See page 90)

LOWE'S TEA ROOMS. George Lowe's grocers shop and tea rooms were situated by Posset Bridge on the corner of Stockport Road and Lockside. They were in a good position to attract trade from the thousands of visitors that came to Marple by train in the first years of this century, when this picture was taken.

SHOP ADVERTISEMENTS, 1902. The shops were promoting themselves in a programme for a 'grand sale of work' to be held by the Albert British Day Schools in their buildings on Church Lane.

RALPH GOULD, PROVISION MERCHANT. The store was on Church Lane opposite Market Street. This magnificent window display from the early 1900s includes an advertisement for his own make of jams.

COMPSTALL POST OFFICE, EARLY 1900s. Children's hoops hang outside the window and a thermometer advertises Stephens' Ink. In the left hand window is a notice: 'Private room for teas and refreshments'. The post office and shop still exist.

LONGHURST LANE, MELLOR. In the early 1900s the shop in the middle of the picture was the post office and general store. It occupied the house next to the recreation field but later 'moved to Moor End'. The cottages and barns on the left were demolished to remove the dangerous bend and widen the road.

LAST DAYS AT MOOR END POST OFFICE, 1995. The post office and store closed at the end of 1995. The last shop in the village, Vivien and Alfred Ayres ran it for eighteen years. Early in the century the local people could buy anything they needed in Moor End from food to clothes, lamp oil to furniture.

Nine

Industry

PEAK FOREST CANAL AND THE RUINS OF THE MINERAL MILL, *c.* 1910.

THOMAS AND JOHN CARVER, *c.* 1900. In 1859 William Carver lent his twin sons, Thomas and John, £15,000 to buy Hollins Mill. With Samuel and Walter Hodgkinson, father and son, they ran the mill and almost every organisation in the village for over fifty years. (See page 77) Thomas and his family lived in Hollins House. After the First World War it was purchased by Marple Urban District Council as their meeting room and offices.

AERIAL VIEW OF HOLLINS MILL, 1950s. The mill, with its six-storey spinning section, extensive single-storey weaving sheds and chimneys, dominated the centre of Marple for over 150 years. (See page 18)

MELLOR MILL AFTER THE FIRE, 1892. The brick built spinning mill built by Samuel Oldknow in the 1790s, was one of the largest in England at that time and employed over 500 people in the early 1800s. Oldknow changed the face of Marple with his involvement in building canals, roads, houses, lime kilns, coal mines and farming.

BOTTOMS HALL, *c.* 1905. Oldknow built Bottoms Hall, now called the Old Hall, to house his mill apprentices. By 1798 there were 100 apprentices, both boys and girls, who worked for thirteen hours a day. By all accounts, judged by the standards of the time, however, he was a good employer. The apprentices were well fed and were given some schooling.

PRIMROSE MILL ON FIRE, MELLOR, 1961. The main building of this mill was burnt down in 1961 when the machinery was being dismantled and removed. The original building may have been used for fulling but in the 1780s, it was enlarged to become one of the earliest muslin yarn producing mills in the area. In the late nineteenth century it produced the yarn for making gas mantles. The remaining part of the buildings is now used by a rubber company.

COMPANY VEHICLES, PRIMROSE MILL, 1950s. These vans were owned by Cropper and Kenyon, who used the mill initially for dying synthetic piece goods and later added screen printing of Terylene dress goods.

MELLOR BLEACHING COMPANY, *c*. 1910s. This letter head shows the bleach works that existed high up the Mill Brow valley at Holly Head until 1926. The first mill on the site was used for cotton spinning. Started in the late 1780s, it changed to bleaching in the middle of the last century. The buildings were demolished shortly after its closure in the early thirties.

SPRINGWATER BLEACH WORKS, TURF LEA, 1920s. This mill is believed to have first been used to grind the roots of the madder plant, used as a red dye, at the Strines Print Works. It was later extended and used at various times as a bleach or print works. Its never failing spring, producing over 40 gallons a minute, was always being mentioned when it was advertised for sale. It was also used for grinding bones. The mill was already in a ruinous condition when it was put up for sale in 1904.

GOYT SPINNING MILL, HAWK GREEN, 1906. Building started in summer 1905 but the mill, although soon in production, was not fully equipped until 1912. By the 1930s it employed 480 people. After it ceased to be used for spinning in the 1960s, it was for a number of years used for the manufacture of plastic foam. It is now subdivided and occupied by a variety of businesses. The chimney, a landmark for many miles, was demolished in the 1980s. (See page 116)

GOYT MILL ENGINES, 1907. This photograph was taken at the commissioning of the engines. The proud staff of the engine room can be seen in front of the enormous wheel that carried the power, by moving ropes, to run the machinery on all the floors of the mill.

COMPSTALL MILL STEAM LORRY. On the occasion of this photograph the men on the carriage, some with rifles, appear to be local volunteers with an officer. Perhaps they were the Compstall Civilian Corps.

MINERAL MILL, EARLY 1900s. A portion of this building still remains on the Strines Road, incorporated into a garage. It stood a little way past the lime kilns, just below the Peak Forest Canal. First built as a corn mill by Samuel Oldknow, it was converted into a mineral mill which processed and ground plaster of Paris, lime and high sulphur coal. It lay derelict for many years after its closure at the start of the century. (See page 107)

THE LIME KILNS, STRINES ROAD, 1950s. These were built by Samuel Oldknow in the late 1780s. They had Gothic style windows to look like a medieval castle from the opposite hillside. The kilns were built into the bank of the canal so that the limestone and coal could be loaded straight into the top, and the lime taken out at the bottom after firing. Workers' dwellings were incorporated into the building. The kilns were abandoned at the start of the century and in the 1960s were reduced to the 'safe' portion that remains today.

GASOMETER, LOWER FOLD, 1976. Newcomers since 1976 will hardly believe that the skyline of Marple Bridge was dominated by an enormous gasometer. (See page 44) The adjoining gas works was privately built in 1845 and was later taken over and run by Marple Council. The site is now occupied by houses.

MARPLE METAL PRODUCTS, SECOND WORLD WAR. The works were on Church Lane, just past the Hatters Arms in the building formerly used as the Gem Cinema. The owners were Pollock McKnabs of Bredbury, who later became Pickups. During the war years they manufactured parts for munitions.

ALFRED GEE, 1977. Up on Ludworth Moor there was, for many years, a 'one man mine'. For over twenty years Alfred Gee worked a ten hour day underground. He sold the coal on site to local people. In the 1970s it became a small open cast mine, closing in 1981. Now that the land has been restored to pasture, it is hard to believe the mine ever existed.

MARPLE RIDGE AND GOYT MILL CHIMNEY, 1960s. The chimney dominated the skyline for miles around. The houses in the foreground are on Windlehurst Lane.

THE END OF HOLLINS MILL CHIMNEY, 1957. The chimney, which had been reduced to ninety feet by steeple jacks, was blown up by 'Blaster' Bates. A large crowd watched as the last of the mill that had been at the centre of Marple for 120 years, fell into a heap of bricks. (See page 108)

Ten

Transport

THE CO-OP BREAD VAN IN THE YARD, MARPLE BRIDGE, *c.* 1920.

PEAK FOREST CANAL. Seen here in the early 1900s, a working boat is just emerging from the tunnel under Station Road, before the widening of the road. A crane to load and unload the boats can be seen by the warehouse on the far side of the bridge. Samuel Oldknow built it to transfer the raw cotton and finished goods between canal and road for his mill situated in the valley below. The original name of St Martin's Road, behind the warehouse, was Wharf Road and it formed the line of the tramway that connected both ends of the Peak Forest Canal before the locks were built.

THE OLD LOCK KEEPER, EARLY 1900s. The name of the lock keeper was George Griffiths and what a face and beard!

MARPLE AQUEDUCT, *c.* 1903. The aqueduct of the Peak Forest Canal, seen in the centre of the picture, was one of the wonders of the Industrial Revolution. Started in 1793, it is 100 feet above the River Goyt, 309 feet long, and took 7 years to build. The railway viaduct towers over it by 24 feet. At the Marple end was the public house called the Queen's Hotel and a mill.

WINTER AT AQUEDUCT COTTAGE, *c.* 1900. The bridge in the centre is the last one before the aqueduct and the house beside it is still there. The canal would often freeze in cold weather, and 'ice breakers' were employed: a small boat was rocked from side to side to break the ice.

POSSETT BRIDGE, c. 1903. Underneath the road there are three tunnels, two for boats and one for the horses who pulled the barges. One was a short arm of the canal leading to the lime kilns; it is now sealed off. (See page 114) The crane was used to unload coal onto the adjacent wharf. The canal smithy, without its chimney, still exists as a house, as does the small building behind the telephone pole. A small parade of shops has since been built between it and the canal.

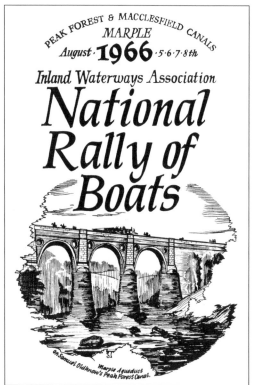

PEAK FOREST & MACCLESFIELD CANALS
MARPLE
August · **1966** · 5·6·7·8th
Inland Waterways Association
National
Rally of
Boats

Wm Samuel Oldknow's Peak Forest Canal.
Marple Aqueduct

POST CARD, 1966. By the mid 1950s the canals had fallen into disrepair and were threatened with closure and being filled in with rubbish. Tremendous efforts were made by volunteers to get the canals 'saved'. In this they were eventually successful and the canals were reopened in 1974. Now, as part of the Cheshire Ring, they are promoted as a tourist attraction by the same organisations that wished to see them closed!

MARPLE STATION IN THE EARLY 1900s. Horse drawn carriages await the arrival of the occupiers of the big Victorian and Edwardian villas to take them home after their day's work at their businesses in Manchester or Stockport. There were direct trains to many places in England, including London, in the heyday of rail travel from Marple.

OLD JOE, 1920s. He is believed to have lived in Compstall and sat outside the station every day.

MARPLE STATION AND BRABYNS BROW. These are the entrances to the station on Brabyns Brow in the early 1900s; more trees overshadowed the road in those days. The station cafe can just be seen on the right hand side. For many years it served the thousands of visitors to the area, as well as the farmers attending the cattle market next door. It still exists and is now the Middlers Restaurant. (See page 87)

MARPLE STATION. The magnificent Victorian station lasted until 1970. On the upper (Manchester) side it had waiting rooms, a stationmaster's house, a booking and parcels office and a footbridge on the up platform that connected directly to Brabyns Brow. There was also a goods siding and shed on the site of what is now the car park. After demolition, the booking office was moved to the lower (New Mills) side.

TOLL HOUSE, ST MARTIN'S ROAD. The gate on the toll road can be seen; it was a private way belonging to Samuel Oldknow. (See page 118) There are no houses on the right hand side, but there is the entrance to Brick Row, the terraced houses that Oldknow built for his workers. These were demolished when Arkwright Road, with its big villas, was constructed in the first few years of this century, when this picture was taken. No new cottages were built for the displaced inhabitants of Brick Row. (See page 38)

CO-OP STABLES, MARPLE BRIDGE, EARLY 1900s. Horses were needed for all the delivery vehicles, including the heavy coal carts. The buildings have only recently been demolished and the site is now occupied by new houses. (See pages 96-98)

MARPLE LADIES' OUTING, *c.* 1925. The coach has solid tyres that must have made for a very bumpy ride!

MELLOR, BAND OF HOPE OUTING, *c.* 1912. Ethel Sigley is seen peeping out from behind the driver on the front seat; Peter Sigley is next to her. Thomas Sigley faces the camera between rows two and three.

THE SECOND BUS ACQUIRED IN 1910. Edith Elizabeth Bridge is sitting beside the driver whilst Francis Joseph Clayton is leaning on the bus.

SHAW'S GARAGE, CHURCH LANE, *c.* 1955. Malcolm Shaw stands at the door of his garage. Since the photograph was taken the garage has been rebuilt, a forecourt constructed, and it no longer sells petrol.

YEATES' GARAGE, STOCKPORT ROAD, 1930s. The garage was substantially altered in recent years but still sells Shell petrol. Now, like most garages, it has a small shop. It even sells lottery tickets!

CHURCH STREET, MARPLE, *c.* 1910. Young ladies line up for the photographer. Two are holding their bicycles; it must have been difficult to ride with those long skirts!

ONE OF MARPLE'S FIRST CARS, *c.* 1930. Miss Edwards of Stonehurst, Hibbert Lane, puts her chauffeur in the back of the car and takes the wheel herself. The battery for the car is on the running board.

Acknowledgments

Mr H.W. Abbott, Mr G. Ardern, Mr M. Arnfield, Mr P. Bardsley, Mr P. Barton, Mrs M. Biddulph, Miss Dawson, the late Mr F. Hawley, Mr H. Hunter, Mr M. Kelly, Mrs L. Mason, Mr G. Mills, Mr F. Myatt, Mrs B. Preston, Mr F. Robinson, Mrs M. Rodway, Mr M. Shaw, Mr W.H. Shercliff, Mrs S. Stokes, Mrs M. Swindells, Mrs D. Walsh, Marple Local History Society, Stockport Heritage Library, the Cromwell Museum and *Cheshire Life*. Thanks are also due to Kirsten Western for her willing help in searching out photographs from the Local History Society's collection.